Children's
333.88
Dickmann
$27

D.

Ser 1 7

THE **FUTURE** OF **POWER**

HARNESSING
GEOTHERMAL
ENERGY

NANCY DICKMANN

PowerKiDS
press.

NEW YORK

Published in 2017 by
The Rosen Publishing Group, Inc.
29 East 21st Street, New York, NY 10010

Cataloging-in-Publication Data

Names: Dickmann, Nancy.
Title: Harnessing geothermal energy / Nancy Dickmann.
Description: New York : PowerKids Press, 2017. | Series: The future of power | Includes index.
Identifiers: ISBN 9781499432114 (pbk.) | ISBN 9781499432299 (library bound) |
    ISBN 9781508153290 (6 pack)
Subjects: LCSH: Geothermal engineering--Juvenile literature. | Geothermal resources--
    Juvenile literature.
Classification: LCC TK1055.D54 2017 | DDC 333.8'8--dc23

For Brown Bear Books Ltd:
Editor: Tim Harris
Editorial Director: Lindsey Lowe
Children's Publisher: Anne O'Daly
Design Manager: Keith Davis
Picture Manager: Sophie Mortimer

Picture Credits: t=top, c=center, b=bottom, l=left, r=right. Interior: 123rf: 13t, 16-17, Alexander Armdt
27, Anthony Brown 9, Johann Ragnarsson 21, Morley Read 25; Dreamtime: 5; Public Domain: GEOMax
Geothermal HVAC Systems 14; Thinkstock: istockphoto 24; US Army: Corps of Engineers 18-19; US
Geological Survey: 8; US Department of Energy: USA.gov 29t, 29inset; Wikipedia: Algkalv 19, Broken Imagery
7, Mike Gonzalez 22, Gretar Ivarsson 13b, RJG Lewis 23, Lydur Skulason 15, StephenG3 10-11.

Manufactured in the United States of America
CPSIA Compliance Information: Batch #BW17PK: For Further Information contact Rosen Publishing, New York, New York at 1-800-237-9932

CONTENTS

HEAT FROM UNDERGROUND

Every time you ride a bus, take a hot shower, heat something in a microwave, or watch television, you are using energy. We use energy in many different forms to power our modern world. We burn fuels in the engines of our vehicles, and we also use them to generate electricity.

For the past several decades, we have relied heavily on coal, oil, and natural gas to meet our energy needs. These fuels are cheap and efficient, but they are running out, and they also cause pollution. In recent years there has been a move toward cleaner, more sustainable forms of energy, such as solar, wind, and hydroelectric power. These types of power rely on natural sources: water, wind, and the Sun. Another type of sustainable energy—geothermal energy—comes from Earth's own heat.

MAKING ELECTRICITY

Geothermal energy is a way of tapping into the natural heat beneath Earth's surface. Engineers have developed ways to use this heat to spin turbines and generate electricity at power stations. It can also be used to heat water, homes, and even roads. Amazingly, geothermal energy can be used to keep homes cool in hot weather!

4

THE BLUE LAGOON

The water in the Blue Lagoon contains a mineral called silica. Sunlight reflecting off the silica makes the water look blue.

THE HOT WATER OF THE BLUE LAGOON IN ICELAND COMES FROM MORE THAN 6,500 FEET (2,000 METERS) UNDERGROUND.

Earth is a sphere made up of several layers, a bit like an onion. The middle part of Earth is the core, which is made of iron and nickel. At the very center, the metals of the core are solid, but the outer core is liquid. The temperature in the core can be up to 10,800 °F (6,000 °C).

Around the core is the mantle. This is a thick layer of rock that is hot enough to behave like a very viscous liquid. The mantle is about 2,550 °F (1,400 °C) in its upper layers. A rocky crust sits on top of the mantle. In some places the crust is only 5 miles (8 km) thick.

In places called "hot spots," the rocks of the upper mantle melt to form magma. The heat of this molten rock can create volcanoes on the surface, as well as other features such as geysers and hot springs.

HOT EARTH

Why is the inside of Earth so hot? First, a lot of heat is still left over from Earth's formation, billions of years ago. Second, the pull of gravity creates heat. Last, some of the radioactive elements deep inside the planet are decaying, and this also produces heat.

OLD FAITHFUL (BELOW) IS A GEYSER IN YELLOWSTONE NATIONAL PARK, WYOMING. IT ERUPTS ABOUT 15 TIMES EVERY DAY.

GEYSERS

When water in Earth's crust comes into contact with hot magma, the water turns to steam. The steam may rise to the surface and shoot up into the air. The fountain of steam and boiling water is a geyser.

HOW DOES IT WORK?

Ancient people knew about natural hot springs, and they used them for bathing and cooking. Sometimes they used them for heating as well. In New Zealand, the native Maori people used hot springs for their health benefits, and so did some Native American tribes. In Europe, the Greeks and Romans used them as spas, bathing in the hot waters. People in the Roman city of Pompeii, on the slopes of an active volcano called Mount Vesuvius, used hot water from underground to heat their buildings.

In the sixteenth and seventeenth centuries, miners looking for minerals started to dig deeper than people had ever gone before. They soon realized that the temperature rises the deeper you go. Before long, a few engineers were able to use natural steam to power pumps and winches. In the early twentieth century, people started to use natural steam to heat buildings and greenhouses.

ROMAN BATHS

Water that has been heated deep underground by geothermal energy fills the ancient baths at Bath, in the United Kingdom. The temperature of the water in the baths is 115°F (46°C).

ANCIENT CHINA

In China, some hot springs have been used since ancient times. Rulers built palaces over the springs. One of the springs became the emperor's bath, with another reserved for palace officials.

ONE OF THE ANCIENT ROMAN BATHS IN THE CITY OF BATH, WHERE HOT WATER RISES TO THE SURFACE THROUGH CRACKS IN ROCKS.

EARLY BEGINNINGS

Once electricity started to light up our cities in the late nineteenth century, engineers looked for new ways to generate it. The first attempt to generate electricity from geothermal steam took place in Italy in 1904, and the generator was able to light four bulbs. In 1911, the first geothermal power plant was built in the same region.

In many different kinds of power plants, electricity is generated when a turbine spins. Wind spins some turbines, and in a hydroelectric plant, the force of moving water is used instead. In most power plants, a fuel such

THE GEYSERS IS A CLUSTER OF 22 GEOTHERMAL PLANTS IN CALIFORNIA. TOGETHER, THEY PRODUCE ELECTRICITY FOR FIVE OF THE STATE'S COUNTIES.

as gas or coal is burned to heat water and create steam. The steam then spins the turbines. A geothermal power station doesn't need to burn fuels because Earth's natural steam does the job.

Geothermal electricity was slow to become popular. The first small geothermal power station opened at Larderello in Italy in 1911, but for many years that country remained the world's only large producer. Then in 1958 a geothermal power station opened in New Zealand, and two years later, the first plant in the United States was built at The Geysers, in California. The Geysers is still one of the largest geothermal plants in the world. Now, there are large geothermal power stations in about a dozen countries around the world, and in some smaller ones as well. More than 25 percent of all the electricity produced in Iceland, the Philippines, and El Salvador is from geothermal energy.

TYPES OF POWER PLANT

There are three main ways of generating electricity using geothermal energy. They all use steam to spin a turbine, but the steam comes from different sources. In a dry steam plant, wells are drilled up to 2 miles (3.2 km) deep to reach reservoirs of steam, which is piped to the surface to spin the turbine. This type of power plant is rare, because there aren't many locations with suitable reservoirs of steam.

The most common type of geothermal power plant is a flash steam station. Instead of steam, the plant's wells allow hot water (at least 360°F, or 182°C) to flow to the surface. The water is piped to a low-pressure tank, where it boils into steam to spin the turbine.

The third type, a binary system, can use cooler water, at temperatures as low as 135°F (57°C). The heat from the water is allowed to transfer to another liquid with a lower boiling point. This second liquid turns to steam to spin the turbine.

BINARY SYSTEMS

Binary systems often use a fluid called butane, which has a very low boiling point. It changes from a liquid to a gas at a temperature as low as 30°F (−1°C).

12

HOT SPOT

Iceland is on a geological hot spot, which gives it volcanoes, geysers, and natural hot springs. About one-third of its electricity—including that used to light its capital, Reykjavik (right)—is generated using geothermal power.

SINCE 1990, NESJAVELLIR GEOTHERMAL POWER STATION IN ICELAND HAS PRODUCED ELECTRICITY AND HOT WATER TO HEAT HOMES.

DIRECT HEATING

Generating electricity from geothermal energy requires high temperatures, which are only found in certain places. However, water at much lower temperatures (as low as 50°F, or 10°C) can be used for heating homes, roads, and sidewalks. Direct heating usually uses water that is less than 1 mile (1.6 km) below the surface, and sometimes as little as a few feet.

In a direct heating system, engineers drill a well down into a geothermal reservoir to provide a steady stream of hot water. The water may be pumped to the surface, or it may flow by itself. A network of pipes takes the hot water where it is needed, and sometimes it flows through a heat exchanger to transfer its heat to another fluid. Once the heat from the water is used, the cooler water is pumped back underground to refill the reservoir.

WARM SIDEWALKS

Iceland may be hot below the ground, but aboveground it is often cold and snowy. The city of Reykjavik has solved this problem by piping hot water from geothermal plants under the roads and sidewalks to melt the snow instead of using snowplows!

A BOREHOLE BENEATH THIS HOUSE CARRIES COOL WATER DEEP UNDERGROUND, WHERE IT IS WARMED AND RISES TO HEAT THE BUILDING.

15

HEAT PUMPS

One of the most common uses of geothermal energy is by installing ground source heat pumps to heat and cool buildings. These pumps take advantage of the temperature below the ground, which stays more or less constant at about 50°F (10°C), all year round. The difference between the temperature aboveground and belowground makes the system work.

A ground source heat pump has a mechanical pump connected to pipes buried in the ground. The pipes form a loop, and the pump helps push air or a fluid— water or another liquid—through the pipes. In winter, when the ground temperature is warmer than the air temperature, the fluid can bring heat up into the building.

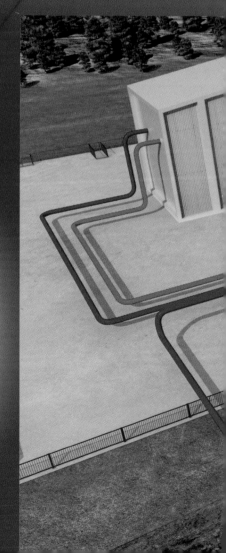

HEAT AND ELECTRICITY

By combining a heat pump system with a binary system—where heat is transferred from water to a fluid with a very low boiling point—it is possible to warm a building and create electricity at the same time.

In the summer, when the air temperature is higher, the pump can take heat from the air back underground, cooling the building.

Many ground source heat pumps need electricity to power the pump. However, for every unit of electricity they use, they can provide up to five times as much energy from the heat underground. Using a ground source heat pump instead of a traditional heating and cooling system can save the average household hundreds of dollars a year.

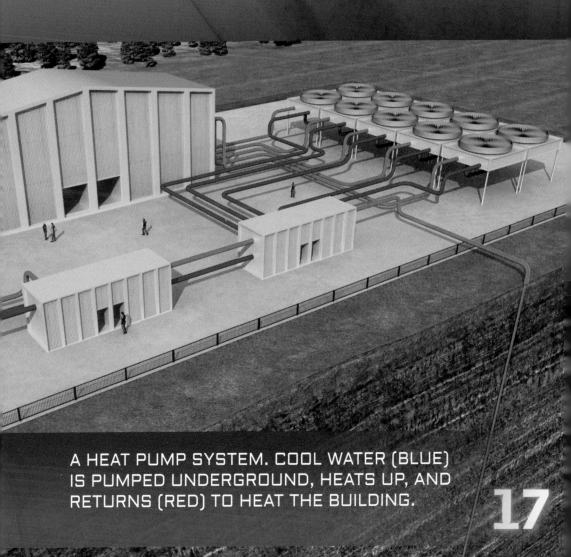

A HEAT PUMP SYSTEM. COOL WATER (BLUE) IS PUMPED UNDERGROUND, HEATS UP, AND RETURNS (RED) TO HEAT THE BUILDING.

GOOD AND BAD

In recent years there has been a big push toward clean, renewable energy. The fossil fuels that have been widely used for decades have two major problems: using them damages the planet, and our supplies are running out. Coal, oil, and natural gas are extracted from reserves underground, but once we exhaust those supplies there will be no more left.

The effect of fossil fuels on the planet is an even bigger problem. Mining coal or drilling for oil and gas can destroy habitats for wildlife, but burning these fuels causes even more damage. They release a gas called carbon dioxide into the atmosphere when they are burned. When large amounts of this gas build up in the atmosphere, it traps the Sun's heat instead of letting it bounce back into space. This makes Earth's average temperature rise, which can cause droughts, melt icecaps, and raise the sea level.

Geothermal energy is both clean and renewable. It comes from Earth's heat, which will not run out for billions of years. Geothermal energy produces very little pollution and has low carbon emissions. A geothermal power plant emits about one-eighth as much carbon dioxide as a coal-fired power plant.

HEATING APARTMENTS

Hot water is drawn from 180 wells bored 650 feet (200 m) under the Nydalen district of Oslo. Heat pumps convert the hot water to hot air, which warms the apartments in winter.

THESE APARTMENTS IN OSLO, NORWAY, ARE HEATED BY GEOTHERMAL ENERGY FROM THE GROUND BENEATH THEM.

19

BENEFITS OF GEOTHERMAL ENERGY

There are many types of renewable energy, including wind and solar power, and they all have their benefits and disadvantages. For example, it is hard to store electricity, so the grid needs a consistent source of power. Wind power can only be used to generate electricity when the wind is blowing, so when it is not blowing other types of power are needed. Geothermal energy doesn't have this problem, because Earth produces heat both day and night, all year round.

Another advantage of geothermal power plants is that they don't take up much space compared to some other types of electricity production. Solar panels at a large power plant can cover acres of land, but geothermal plants are usually much smaller. At least some of the hardware is usually buried underground. This means that geothermal power plants leave more land available for farming, building homes, or wildlife.

Flexibility is another advantage. Geothermal power can be used for generating electricity in large power plants, but an installation doesn't have to be big to be efficient. Geothermal power can also be used for more than just generating electricity. For example, it can provide heating and cooling—for a whole town or for just a single house.

EXPORTING ELECTRICITY?
Iceland could produce more electricity from geothermal energy than it needs to light its homes and run its industries. There are plans for an underwater cable to carry surplus electricity to the United Kingdom.

A GEOTHERMAL POWER STATION IN ICELAND AT NIGHT. UNLIKE SOLAR AND WIND ENERGY, GEOTHERMAL ENERGY IS ALWAYS AVAILABLE.

21

THE PHILIPPINES IS THE WORLD'S SECOND
MOST IMPORTANT PRODUCER OF GEOTHERMAL
ENERGY, AFTER THE UNITED STATES. THIS IS
THE PUHAGAN GEOTHERMAL POWER STATION.

LOCATION AND COST

With all the advantages, you might think that geothermal would be one of our main energy sources. But in fact, it makes up less than 1 percent of the energy used around the world. One of the main reasons for this is location. In many places on Earth, the geothermal reservoirs are just too difficult and expensive to reach. Only a small number of countries, such as Iceland and the Philippines, are able to produce a lot of electricity from geothermal. However, there are many more locations where geothermal power can be used directly for heating.

Another problem with geothermal energy is its cost. Setting up a ground source heat pump for a single home can cost several thousand dollars. It might take more than 10 years for the savings in energy bills to pay back the cost of installing the system. Many people just can't afford this.

DRILLING A WELL

Drilling a new well for a geothermal power plant is a big job, since the well may need to be more than 1 mile (1.6 km) deep. Drilling can cost millions of dollars, which has to be spent before the power plant can start making money by selling electricity.

23

ENVIRONMENT AND IMPACT

Harnessing geothermal energy can have an impact on the environment. The process usually involves bringing water to the surface, either as a liquid or as steam. In one installation in New Zealand, the loss of underground water has led to the land above it sinking. In many geothermal systems, the water that is brought up is pumped back into the ground.

Engineers are trying out a new technique called the Enhanced Geothermal System (EGS). This can be used where there are hot rocks underground, but not enough water or steam to use for traditional geothermal power. In an EGS, fluid is pumped into deep wells, where it can heat up and then return to the surface to be used. However, studies have shown that this can sometimes cause small earthquakes.

CLEANER ENERGY

Some types of geothermal power plants bring gases from underground to the surface. Some of the gases are toxic, and others cause global warming. However, the amount of gases released is much lower than from power plants that burn fossil fuels.

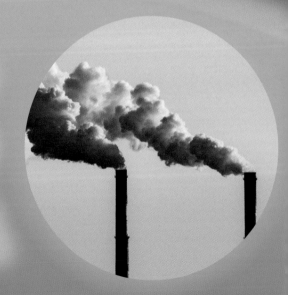

ROADS ARE BUILT TO REACH GEOTHERMAL INSTALLATIONS. IF THE ROADS CUT THROUGH FORESTS, THEY MAY DAMAGE VALUABLE HABITATS.

25

THE FUTURE

Scientists estimate that the heat in the top 6 miles (9.6 km) or so of Earth's crust has 50,000 times as much energy as all of our oil and natural gas resources! Finding a way to use this heat in an efficient, cost-effective way is a challenge for the future.

Our need for cheap, reliable energy that doesn't pollute the planet means that geothermal energy is becoming more important. Unlike solar and wind power, it can provide reliable, constant electricity, both day and night. More and more people are installing ground source heat pumps in their homes (about 60,000 each year in the United States), but geothermal is still a long way from taking over from fossil fuels.

Scientists believe that geothermal power has the potential to produce 8.3 percent of the world's electricity in the near future. Experts have identified 39 countries that may be able to produce all their electricity requirements through geothermal power.

Technology is constantly improving, which will make geothermal energy cheaper to produce. New techniques also mean that more and more locations have the potential to produce geothermal power.

MOUNT BROMO IS AN ACTIVE VOLCANO IN INDONESIA. VOLCANIC AREAS HAVE PLENTIFUL GEOTHERMAL ENERGY, BUT IT IS HARD TO HARNESS.

27

NEW METHODS

Many of the best, most efficient locations for geothermal power plants are already being used. In order to expand the production of geothermal energy, we need to find new ways of harnessing it. These will allow more and more areas to produce geothermal power.

One important tecÚique is an Enhanced Geothermal System, which pumps water down wells to heat up. The heated water can be used either for direct heating (in homes, greenhouses, or other locations) or for generating electricity.

Another promising tecÚology combines geothermal with fossil fuels. When engineers dig wells to extract oil and gas, they often find hot water suitable for producing geothermal electricity. At the moment, most of this hot water just goes to waste. If drilling companies started to harness it, they could generate electricity at the same time as they extract oil and gas. New ideas like this will make geothermal power a big part of our energy future.

FOUR STATES
Most geothermal energy in the United States is generated in the states of California, Nevada, Utah, and Hawaii. Together, they produce as much electricity as three large nuclear power stations.

DEEPER AND HOTTER

The deeper you go into Earth's crust, the hotter it gets. Many geothermal wells are 1 to 1.5 miles (1.6 to 2.4 km) deep. A project in Iceland is testing much deeper wells, 2 to 3 miles (3.2 to 4.8 km) deep. The rocks and fluids in these deep wells are much hotter and can generate more electricity.

29

GLOSSARY

boiling point: The temperature at which a fluid changes from a liquid to a gas.

fluid: A substance that tends to flow and conform to the shape of its container; a liquid or a gas.

fossil fuels: Fuels such as coal, oil, and natural gas that are the buried remains of plants and animals that lived long ago.

global warming: An increase in the average temperature of Earth's atmosphere.

gravity: The force that attracts a physical object to the center of Earth or toward another physical body with mass.

grid: A power transmission network taking electricity from where it is generated to where it is needed.

mineral: A naturally occurring solid that does not come from an animal or plant. Every mineral is made up of a particular mix of chemical elements.

pollution: The release of substances that have harmful or toxic effects into the atmosphere, rivers, or oceans.

radioactive: Describing elements that give off rays of energy or particles (radiation) when atoms break apart.

turbine: A machine with blades attached to a central rotating shaft. Turbines are used to generate electricity.

viscous: Thick or sticky.

FURTHER INFORMATION

BOOKS

Brennan, Linda. *Geothermal Power.* North Mankato, MN: Cherry Lake Publishing, 2013.

Challoner, Jack. *Energy* (Eyewitness). NY: Dorling Kindersley, 2012.

Doeden, Matt. *Finding Out about Geothermal Energy.* Minneapolis, MN: Lerner Classroom, 2014.

WEBSITES

Due to the changing nature of Internet links, PowerKids Press has developed an online list of websites related to the subject of this book. This site is updated regularly. Please use this link to access the list:

www.powerkidslinks.com/tfop/geo

INDEX